STORIES OF METHODIST MUSIC

STORIES OF
METHODIST MUSIC

By

JAMES T. LIGHTWOOD

Author of 'Hymn Tunes and their Story,' 'Methodist Music
of the Eighteenth Century,' 'Dickens and Music,' &c.

London
THE EPWORTH PRESS
J. ALFRED SHARP

First Edition, 1928.

Made and Printed in Great Britain by
Rush & Warwick, Harpur Printing Works, Bedford.

CONTENTS

Stories of Methodist Music

CHAPTER I

THE EARLY HYMN-BOOKS

John Wesley's Hymn-Book.

A MONGST the many treasures bequeathed to his followers by John Wesley there are two that are of special interest to students of hymnology and church music. The output of hymn pamphlets and collections of hymns flowed from the Wesley press in ever-increasing numbers, and it must have been difficult for the good Methodists of the eighteenth century to know exactly which special edition or collection they should take with them when going forth to the Sunday service. It does not appear to have been the custom in those days to provide hymn-books at the preaching-houses ' For Visitors only,' and worshippers, or at any rate those of them who could read, were supposed to bring hymn-books with them.

With a view to simplify the somewhat complicated conditions arising out of such an extensive choice, Wesley took the matter in hand, or, to use the words of his famous Preface, ' I have been importuned to publish such a HYMN-BOOK as might be generally used in all our Congregations throughout Great Britain and Ireland.' The result of his work appeared in 1780 under the title *A Collection of Hymns for the Use of the People Called Methodists.*

This remained the standard hymn-book for Methodist congregations for half a century. During that period at least thirty-eight editions were published (not including ' pirated ' ones), and in the course of years many deviations were made from Wesley's original scheme. His own final revision was ' The Third Edition corrected,' 1782; and this was reproduced in facsimile in 1904.

In the fifth edition (1786), which would be published with Wesley's approval, an important addition was made, the name of a suitable tune selected from *Sacred Harmony* (1780) being added above each hymn. Wesley evidently approved of the 'fixed tune' system, and would doubtless feel he had done all he could to prevent irresponsible leaders of the singing from introducing new tunes composed by themselves or their friends.

Wesley's Last Tune-Book.

This hymn-book and its accompanying tune-book (*Sacred Harmony*) provided all that was necessary for the Methodist service of praise for many a long year. In 1882 a new oblong edition of *Sacred Harmony* was published under the editorship of Charles Wesley, who, on the title-page, proudly inscribed himself as the 'nephew' of John Wesley. No further tune-book was published by the authority of Conference till 1876.

'Come, let us anew.'

Few hymns have more sacred associations than the one with which Methodist congregations invariably welcome the birth of another year. There is one tune, and one tune only, that is now associated with it, and the union has become hallowed by the custom of many generations. So well are hymn and tune fitted to each other, that one is inclined to ask who is responsible for the association.

In the Conference Library there is a copy of the fourth edition of *Sacred Melody* (1761). Published in 1773, this particular issue has become singularly scarce; and additional value is given to this Library copy, owing to the fact that it was the one which John Wesley corrected with his own hand when preparing to issue his *Sacred Harmony* (1780).

The hymn 'Come, let us anew' was originally set to a melody which has long since disappeared. It was called 'New Year's Day,' and, whatever may have been its merits, it seems that Wesley did not think it suitable, or it may be that a new tune, which he had picked up somewhere—no one now knows where—would prove a more appropriate setting. So we find that in his copy of *Sacred Melody* he has crossed out 'New Year's Day' and written above it 'Derby,' and thus it is to him we are indebted for the choice of a tune which has for long been the great New Year's song for Methodist congregations.

New Regulations.

Not until five years after the death of John Wesley do we find at the various Conferences any reference to singing or to music generally. However, in 1796 the old resolution concerning the singing of anthems underwent a slight modification, and was reproduced in this form :

' Let no anthems be introduced into our chapels (unless on extraordinary occasions and with the consent of the Assistant) because they cannot properly be called joint-worship.

' Also we agree with our late Rev. Father that our own tunes should be learned and sung in preference to others, as in these the whole congregation can in general join.'

That anthem singing was a feature at the Methodist chapels, at any rate in the North of England and the Midlands, is shown by the publication in 1797 of a small pamphlet with the title :

FAVORITE HYMNS,
ODES AND ANTHEMS,
AS SUNG AT
THE METHODIST CHAPELS
IN THE
SHEFFIELD, ROTHERHAM, DONCASTER,
AND NOTTINGHAM CIRCUITS.

———

THE FIFTH EDITION, IMPROVED
BY J. WILDE.
PRINTED IN THE YEAR 1797.
PRICE TWOPENCE.

As this was the ' Fifth ' edition, it is safe to assume that this little anthem-book was already widely used. The compiler was leader of the singing at Norfolk Street Chapel, Sheffield, and he bears excellent testimony to the worth of his choir in these words : ' I do not consider it to be any violation of the laws of truth to observe that Congregational Harmony is better performed among the Methodists at *Norfolk Street Chapel* than in any other place of worship in Sheffield or its vicinity.' We also learn from Wilde's Preface that the anthems were not only for the use of the choir, but were to be sung by any of the congregation who could join in. ' Let those persons ' (wrote this choir-leader) ' who are dispersed throughout the chapel, and who sing the bass part, use the same notes they hear from the singers; inattention to this produces discord. Secondly, keep time with the singers, that is to say, go not before nor hang behind them; both of which cause disorder.

' Lastly, and above all things, let not the men sing in the repeats, which the women take; this destroys the beauty, simplicity, and excellency for which Methodist singing has been so long celebrated.'

The direction that those who sang bass were to take their notes from the singers would scarcely be conducive to strict time being kept in the performance of the music. The reason for the suggestion probably was that copies of the music existed in manuscript only, and there would not be any available except for the singers' pew.

CHAPTER II

EARLY METHODIST ANTHEMS

THE selections in Wilde's pamphlet referred to in the last chapter are all of the ' hymn-anthem ' species. The composers include James Leach of Roihdale, Luke Procter (an amateur musician in Sheffield), and W. E. Miller, son of Dr. Miller, the famous organist of Doncaster Parish Church. Wilde left Sheffield in 1798, and subsequently became leader of the singing at City Road Chapel. A year later W. E. Miller, who was a regular attendant at Norfolk Street Chapel, entered the Wesleyan ministry; but, as we shall see later, he did not allow his ministerial work to interfere with his love of music.

Miller was not the only preacher who contributed to the music of the Church. A famous predecessor was Thomas Olivers, who has a double claim on us, for he was the composer of ' Helmsley ' and also the author of ' The God of Abraham praise.' The statement frequently made that ' Helmsley ' is founded on a hornpipe is entirely wrong, and has been disproved again and again. Previous reference has been made to the Rev. John Beaumont, whose anthems, though forgotten to-day, had a wonderful vogue at the beginning of the last century.

More Regulations.

Thus we see that the practice of singing anthems in the Methodist chapels was becoming an established custom. Conference, however, viewed its growth with alarm, and a further effort was made to stay the tide. During 1797 the various rules and regulations that had appeared from time to time in what were known as the *Large Minutes* were revised and accepted by Conference as authoritative. These were published as a *Collection of Rules, or Code of Laws,* and here we find that the resolutions of the various Conferences from 1746 in reference to music are epitomized under the heading ' How to guard against formality in public worship, especially in singing.'

Q. 20. How shall we guard against formality in public worship?

A. 1. By carefully warning the people against it. By taking care that our own minds are duly affected by the truths we preach; never losing sight of ourselves.

2. By choosing such hymns as are suitable to the congregation. By singing not too much at once, seldom more than five or six verses. By suiting the tune to the words. By sometimes seriously asking the people, ' Now, do you know what you said last? Did you speak no more than you felt? '

3. Is not formality in singing creeping in, singing those complex tunes and anthems which it is scarcely possible to sing with devotion? The repeating the same words so often, and especially while another is repeating other words (the horrid abuse which runs through the modern church music), as it shocks all common sense, so it necessarily brings in dead formality and has no religion in it. Besides, it is a flat contradiction to our Lord's command, ' Use not vain repetitions '; for what is a vain repetition, if this is not? What end of devotion does it serve? Sing no anthems.

4. Do not suffer the people to sing too slow; this naturally tends to formality. In every large Society let them learn to sing; and let them always learn our own tunes first. Let the women constantly sing their own parts alone; let no man sing with them, unless he understands the notes and sings the bass. Introduce no new tunes till they are perfect in the old ones.

5. Let no organ be placed anywhere, till it be proposed at the Conference. Recommend the Tune-Book everywhere; and if you cannot sing yourself, choose a person or two in each place to pitch the tune for you. Exhort every one, whether man or woman, in the congregation, to sing. If a Preacher be present, let no other person give out the words. When they wish to teach the congregation to sing any new tune, they should only sing the tenor.

EARLY METHODIST ANTHEMS

The only other reference in these epitomized *Rules* that concerns our story is found under the heading, ' The most useful way of preaching ' : ' Everywhere avail yourselves of the great festivals, by preaching on the occasion, and singing our hymns, which you should take care to have in readiness.'

No Anthems to be Sung.

Here, then, we have the attitude of Conference towards music and singing at the close of the eighteenth century. Put briefly, we find that

1. No anthems were to be sung.
2. No organs allowed without the sanction of Conference.
3. Great attention was to be paid to the singing.

It is very difficult to discover what the particular anthems were to which the Conference took objection, since there are but few records of the special music which the choir-leaders availed themselves of. At the opening of King Street Chapel, Bristol, in 1795, the anthems were: ' Let the righteous rejoice before God,' ' O Zion that bringest good things,' ' Lift up your heads,' ' The Hallelujah Chorus.'

The last three, from *Messiah,* may have been amongst those ' pieces ' which came under the ban, though Wesley had some years before expressed approval of Handel's music. He heard the oratorio at Bristol Cathedral in 1758, and has recorded that ' In many parts, especially several of the choruses, it exceeded my expectation.'

It is safe to assume that the objection taken by Conference to the singing of anthems, which, as we have seen, was first mentioned in 1787, was founded on Wesley's own experiences, and there is plenty of evidence to show that his decisions, at any rate on musical subjects, were accepted as final by his brethren.

The opening of the nineteenth century discloses much activity amongst the singers and choir-leaders in Methodist chapels, and it is evident that the exhortations of the Conference were being carefully attended to. It was the custom in many places to engage teachers of singing to train the people, and records of payments to them appear in some of the old account-books, as, for instance, at Liverpool, where 5s. 6d. was paid ' to Mr. Marsden as a gratuity to learn the singers.' Special provision was made for a seat for the singers when new preaching-houses were erected. We have already seen that organs had been admitted in the chapels at Bath, Newark, and Keighley; but the only instrument that had official recognition was the bass fiddle. The presence of these instruments sufficiently disproves the story that Wesley, on being asked if he disapproved of musical instruments in a place of worship, replied that he had no objection to instruments of music in a place of worship ' provided they were neither seen nor heard.' The story is purely apocryphal, and may safely be consigned to oblivion.

In a few places attention was paid to the comfort of the singers. For instance, we find that half a guinea was paid for carpet for the singers' seat at Norfolk Street Chapel, Sheffield. The Methodists of this town seem to have been very kindly disposed towards their singers, and they did not hesitate to make a money grant towards choir expenses. Norfolk Street Chapel was particularly proud of its bass fiddle, which had passed with them from the old chapel in Mulberry Street, and it remained their one and only instrument of music till the erection of the first organ in 1860.

CHAPTER III

AN OLD ANTHEM-BOOK

THE publication of Wilde's anthem-book seems to suggest that Methodist musicians did not find full scope for their powers and their ambitions in the words of the collection of hymns that Wesley had bequeathed to them. Not that they found any fault with the sentiments so poetically expressed therein; but what they complained of was, in effect, that the severe and somewhat inelastic form of the hymn-tune did not provide enough opportunity for musical effect on great occasions.

Moreover, the choice of music was decidedly limited; that is, if singers confined their attention to the collection in *Sacred Harmony*, which was, or at any rate which was supposed to be, their official guide in the matter of suitable music. That collection contained one hundred and twenty tunes, and doubtless the singers did not think that they afforded sufficient variety for a hymn-book which contained more than four times as many hymns. Was there ever any attempt to go outside these authorized collections of hymns and music, and provide some needful variety to sustain the interest and musical instincts of the singers?

The answer to this question is found not only in this Sheffield anthem-book of Wilde's which has already been described, but also in another scarce pamphlet, also of Yorkshire origin, the place of its birth being Hull. It bears the title

HYMNS selected from various authors; to be sung at the
METHODIST CHAPEL, George Yard, Hull.
Printed by W. Cowley, Hull. 1798.
Price twopence.

The Introduction to this little collection of twenty-seven hymns

15

or ' pieces ' is so interesting, and throws such a light on the conditions that prevailed in those days, that I have no hesitation in reproducing it.

TO THE READER.

The design of this small collection of Hymns is, that those detached pieces of music which are frequently sung in the Methodist Chapel in George Yard, before Sermons, may be more generally understood, which cannot fail of being accomplished in those who have any taste for sacred Music, when they have the words in their Hands, they may with ease attend to and obtain a perfect knowledge of the Tunes, so that in a very short time they will be generally sung throughout the Congregation at large.

Singing the praise of God in the great congregation is the highest employment the children of men can be engaged in, here upon earth; it comes the nearest (so far as we can judge), to the employment of angels and arch-angels, cherubin and seraphin, and the spirits of the just made perfect in the heavenly state. It is calculated both to spiritualize the affections and to impress the memory at the same time.

As a part of divine worship, it becomes the duty of all Christians to perform the same in the most acceptable manner possible. That this part of the worship of Almighty God may be performed to His Glory and the edification of His Church, I take the present opportunity to propose two or three things to the Congregation, which, if attended to, will greatly contribute to remove those improprieties which have occasioned discord, and deservedly brought reproach upon us. First, let the Congregation at large give strict attention to the Leader, and the singers in the singing Pew, and be careful neither to go before nor to lag behind; in either case discord must be the consequence.

Secondly. Let all the women who can, strive to sing (not one in ten only) the repeats or the parts allotted to them.

And Thirdly. See that the men never join in the women's part (except they can sing the Bass with Propriety). To do this,

AN OLD ANTHEM-BOOK

is to destroy the beauty, simplicity and excellency, for which the Methodist Congregations in general, and those in Yorkshire in particular, have been so justly admired.

Hull, 1798.   T. H.

It would be interesting to know whom these initials represent. He certainly was not one of the trustees, as there is no name to fit them in the list given in W. H. Thompson's records of the George Yard Chapel. Nor was he a minister, as the two who were stationed at Hull in 1798 were Joseph Benson (who was President of the Conference that year) and Robert Lomas. In the Wesleyan Conference Library there is an autobiography of Benson, which still remains in manuscript carefully bound in four large volumes. There is no reference in this to the services at George Yard, nor do we find any intimation as to who T.H. was. Probably it is quite safe to assume that he was the leader of the singing at the chapel, and the publication of the pamphlet is sufficient evidence of his desire to add new interest to the musical part of the service.

Here is a list of the pieces in this book. In each case the words are given in full. This seems to suggest that the book was intended for the use of the congregation. It will be seen that some of the pieces were known by titles, as well as by the first line of the hymn :—

1. ' Come, Thou Soul-transforming Spirit.' 2. ' Beyond the glittering, starry sky.' 3. The Fall of Babylon : ' In Gabriel's hand a mighty stone.' 4. ' Jerusalem divine! ' 5. ' At Jacob's well a stranger sought.' 6. Hosannah : ' Come, angels! seize your harps of gold.' 7. The Promised Land : ' Happy beyond description he.' 8. The Pilgrim's song : ' Rise, my soul, and stretch thy wings.' 9. ' Hail, happy day, a day of holy rest.' 10. ' He dies, the Friend of sinners dies.' 11. On the sufferings of Christ : ' Thou soft flowing Kedron.' 12. The Methodist Parting : ' Our souls, by love together knit.' 13. Before sermon : ' In boundless mercy, gracious Lord, appear.' 14. ' All hail the pow'r of Jesu's name! ' 15 : ' Our Lord is risen from the dead.'

17

16. ' Vital spark of heavenly flame.' 17. Barren Fig Tree : ' Although the Fig Tree shall not blossom.' 18. ' Plung'd in a gulph of dark despair.' 19. ' Before Jehovah's awful throne.' 20. ' Hail, hail, revive, reviving spring.' 21. ' My God, the spring of all my joys.' 22. ' From all that dwell below the skies.' 23. ' Not all the blood of beasts, on Jewish altars slain.' 24. ' Father, how wide Thy glory shines.' 25. ' Great source from whom all blessings flow.' 26. ' O Thou God of my salvation.' 27. Dismission : ' Lord, dismiss us with Thy blessing.'

None of these was in the Hymn-book then in use, though three of them (10, 15, and 21) were included in a *Supplement* added in 1803. To many of them a refrain or chorus is added, and in some cases the name of the composer of the music is given. W. E. Miller is responsible for 6, 11, and 12, and possibly for the words of No. 6. Every one of the pieces is in hymn-anthem form except No. 17, the words of which are taken from the third chapter of Habakkuk, set to music by John Beamont.

Three of the anthems (16, 19, and 20) had long been favourites. We have already seen how impressed Wesley was with the music of ' Vital spark,' when he heard it sung by a choir of fifty children at Bolton. ' Before Jehovah's awful throne ' is a striking example of how singularly effective simple yet well-written music can be. Composed by Martin Madan about the middle of the eighteenth century, it is still to be heard in some places, and forms an important link between the past and the present in our Church music.

CHAPTER IV

MORE ABOUT THE OLD ANTHEMS

THERE are a few more anthems in the George Yard pamphlet which merit further comment. No. 25 is a sad example of what some 'hymn-menders' are capable of. In 1792 the Rev. T. Haweis, who, besides being one of Lady Huntingdon's chaplains, was also a poet and composer, published at Bath a collection of original hymns and music called *Carmina Christo*. One of the hymns commenced with the verse

> O Thou from whom all goodness flows,
> I lift my heart to Thee;
> In all my sorrows, conflicts, woes,
> Dear Lord, remember me.

The music of this hymn is the well-known tune 'Richmond,' and it originally ended with a refrain. It was doubtless this fact that commended it to 'T.H.'s' notice when making his selection for the George Yard Methodists; but for some unknown reason the hymn is printed in a strangely disguised form, the first verse being

> Great Source from whom all blessings flow,
> To Thee for help I flee;
> In all my complicated woe,
> O Lord! remember me.

The other verses receive similar treatment, and a curious perversion is the result.

In the preface to his *Carmina Christo*, Haweis, who was at one time rector of Oldwinkle, Northamptonshire, gives a sad picture of the state of the music in a country church in his days. He says:

' Even in our public worship the voice of joy and gladness is too commonly silent, unless in that shameful mode of psalmody, now almost confined to the wretched solo of a parish clerk, or to a few persons huddled together in one corner of the church, who sing to the praise and glory of themselves, for the entertainment, or oftener for the weariness of the rest of the congregation—an absurdity too glaring to be overlooked, and too shocking to be ridiculous! '

Seagrave's hymn (No. 8) owed its long popularity both to its own merits, and also, in no small degree, to the somewhat rampant and rollicking music which some unknown composer wrote for it. The metre of the hymn is that known as ' sevens and sixes,' or ' Kingswood measure,' and in setting it to music the composer, who christened his tune ' Dartford,' gave full reins to his fancy. Here is the first verse of the hymn which, by the way, never found its way into a Methodist collection :

> Rise, my soul, and stretch thy wings,
>   Thy better portion trace,
> Rise from transitory, things
>   Tow'rds heav'n, thy native place.
> Sun and moon and stars decay,
>   Time shall soon this earth remove;
> Rise, my soul, and haste away,
>   To seats prepared above.

In his music the composer repeated the third and fourth lines; and then, having set the fifth line, he embarked on a series of repeats, with this result :

Time shall soon this, Time shall soon this, Time shall soon this earth remove;
Rise my soul and Rise my soul and Rise my soul and haste away,

and then the music comes to a triumphant conclusion. With a view to securing a suitable rendering of his strains, the composer has given directions for soft and loud singing alternately, which may tend to give variety to the music, resulting, however, in a total disregard of the significance of the words. ' Dartford ' is certainly an extreme example of vain repetitions, though it by no means stands alone.

James Leach, of Rochdale.

Perhaps the most famous of the composers whose music was

sung at this George Yard Chapel is James Leach, whose 'Promised Land' (No. 7) is a setting of one of Wesley's hymns for children, arranged for duet and chorus. This Lancashire composer's music had a long run of popularity, and his memory is still treasured by those who have heard or sung his tunes and anthems. His music was greatly loved by Methodist singers, and he certainly deserves a prominent place in our story.

James Leach was born in the village of Wardle, near Rochdale, in a small cottage close to the Methodist chapel, in which he subsequently commenced his successful career. The village was a musical one, and it was amongst ' players on the fiddle, clarionet, flute, blowers, horseleg, and serpent wrostlers, players on the brass trumpet, and singers,' that the youngster spent his early years. Of all these musicians the most famous was Isaac Bamford, known generally as ' Owd Isaac '; and the boy's joy was unbounded when the great man undertook to give him lessons. At first young Leach did not evince much curiosity about musical terms and phrases, but as he grew older his interest was awakened, and the questions he put to his tutor on the subject of fugue, part writing, and other mysteries pertaining to the art, greatly puzzled Owd Isaac, who began to find that he was being taken out of his depth. Whilst he was busy at the loom, Leach did not neglect his music, and when he reached his eighteenth year he began to compose, his first effort being a setting of the hymn ' The Lord my pasture shall prepare.' Soon after his marriage he showed some of his tunes to his wife, and their merits were carefully discussed by the young couple. Leach did not imagine that a humble musician born in a little place like Wardle could ever take rank with ' those great folk as can make music live for hundreds o' years.'

' Why not,' argued his wife, who pointed out that every musician had to be born somewhere, and what was the matter with Wardle? At last Leach made up his mind. He prepared band parts of his tunes, and got the local musicians to play them, the result being that his fame soon began to be spread abroad. Tunes like ' Mount Pleasant,' ' Pisgah,' and ' Oldham ' struck a new note in psalmody, and the graceful outlines of the melodies made a prompt appeal. It is on record that in the spring of 1788 John Wesley visited the village, and after holding a service he asked where the tunes they sang came from, and who the composer was, as he had never heard them before. Leach's uncle, who was a Methodist local preacher, introduced his nephew to Wesley, who praised his work, and spoke kind words of encouragement to him.

The young musician had now come to the parting of the ways; and after carefully considering his chances, he relinquished his occupation in the weaving-shed and commenced a new career as a professor of music. A great farewell ' sing ' was organized in his native village, his own compositions filling the programme, and off went Leach and his wife to take up their residence in Rochdale.

One would scarcely look in the *Arminian Magazine* of those days for musical paragraphs, nor would one expect its three leaves of advertisements to help the historian of music. It was therefore a pleasant surprise, on searching the pages of the late eighteenth-century volumes, to find useful information about Leach and his tune-books. There were good reasons for using the *Magazine* for advertising purposes, for it had a very wide circulation in the towns and villages of the land; so that Leach was therefore well advised to advertise his musical productions therein. The first collection of his compositions, which he called *A New Sett of Psalm and Hymn Tunes,* entered the world unannounced in 1789, the Preface being dated from Rochdale.

CHAPTER V

SOME EARLY PSALMODISTS

Leach's Hymn-Tunes.

JAMES LEACH'S first volume of original tunes did not meet with the success he had hoped for; in fact, it took six years to exhaust the edition, and then, finding there was still a demand for the book, Leach decided to resort to advertisement to try to secure a more rapid sale. His first advertisement appeared in *The Arminian Magazine* for December 1795, when we find the second edition of the *New Sett* announced, the composer describing himself as ' Conductor of the singers belonging to the Methodist Chapels in Manchester.'

The announcement informs us that ' the greater part of these tunes were designedly composed for the use of the Methodist congregations, in that much esteemed mode of singing, where the women take the piano parts, accompanied by the bass only. This method was highly approved of, and continually encouraged by our late reverend Father, Mr. Wesley; and it is hoped that, ere long, it will become universal in all the Methodist chapels and places of worship, as every lover of sacred Music must unavoidably give it the preference to the common way, where the tenor voices accompany the treble in repeats, and other piano parts.'

After informing the public that the first edition of his *Tunes* was chiefly disposed of in Lancashire and Yorkshire, he announces that ' if his Life is spared ' he will shortly issue a *Second Sett of Psalm and Hymn Tunes.* This duly appeared in 1796, the composer being assisted financially in his undertaking by a Rochdale manufacturer named James Hamilton. During his residence in Rochdale Leach conducted the choir at the Wesleyan chapel in Union Street, and he also obtained a large connexion as a teacher of music. In 1795 he moved with his family to Salford; but he had not been there long before his career was closed by a fatal accident. He had been visiting Rochdale, and on his return to Manchester the coach was overturned in descending Blackley Brow, the passengers being all thrown out. None of them was injured except Leach, who was found lying dead in the road, holding a broken fiddle case containing Owd Isaac's fiddle. He was buried in the yard of Union Street Chapel, Rochdale, and a memorial stone was erected over his grave, on which was carved his beautiful minor melody 'Egypt.' A few years ago his memory was honoured by the erection of a memorial tablet in the same sanctuary. The fame of his hymn-tunes had already carried his name across to America, and in the very year that he died we find some of his compositions in *The Easy Instructor*, a collection of tunes published at Albany, U.S.A., in 1798.

Two or three years later a volume containing many of Leach's anthems was published, and these provided standard works for special occasions for many years. The volume was advertised in *The Arminian Magazine* for May 1802, where it is announced as being published in twelve parts, at half-a-crown each, the price being raised sixpence a number owing to the extravagant price of paper.

William Arnold, and others.

It is rather curious that Leach's tunes, once so popular, have not survived the passing of the years. There is scarcely one to be found in modern tune-books, and his name is nearly forgotten save in the neighbourhood where he first became known. Some of his contemporaries have been more fortunate: William Arnold, composer of 'Josiah,' 'Job,' and 'Sarah,' was a shipwright in H.M. Dockyard at Portsmouth. For some years he was leader of the choir at the Methodist Chapel in Daniel Street, Portsea. He published a collection of his compositions, containing fifty-four tunes, in addition to those mentioned above. 'Job' has recently obtained a new lease of life, being sung to 'When I survey the wondrous cross.' But, needless to say, it has not displaced 'Rockingham' as the standard tune

SOME EARLY PSALMODISTS

for Dr. Watts's famous hymn. Most of the tunes in the appendix to the *Methodist Hymn-Book* date from the early years of last century, and contemporaneous with Arnold were Isaac Tucker (' Devizes '), Phillips of Bristol (' New Sabbath '), John Eagleton (' Justification '), Samuel Stanley of Birmingham (' Warwick ' and ' Simeon '), and T. Howgate of Manchester whose well-known tune, ' Worsley,' still retains its popularity.

On the back of the cover of *The Arminian Magazine* for January 1805 appears this advertisement :

SACRED MUSIC.

Just published, price 4/6.

A set of Psalm and Hymn-Tunes, with some select pieces, and an anthem, principally adapted for the singers of Dissenting Congregations. The music in four parts, and figured for the organ, pianoforte, &c.

By Thomas Clark, Canterbury.

The above may be had of Mr. Lomas, City Road, by applying to any of the Preachers.

Little is known of this composer. He seems to have been a Canterbury man, and the fact that his tunes were to be had at the Book Room in City Road seems to confirm the statement that he was at one time leader of the choir at the Methodist Chapel in Canterbury. He led an active life, and was concerned in the publication of several books of psalmody. Some of his tunes lived through the century, nor are they yet altogether forgotten. A curious fate has befallen one of his best-known tunes, ' Cranbrook,' at one time the recognized setting of ' Grace, 'tis a charming sound.' Having fulfilled its mission in the sanctuary, it has passed into the secular world, and is now sung with much vigour to a poetical version of an old Yorkshire story known as ' On Ilka Moor 'baht Hat '!

There is no doubt that these old choir-leaders took a keen interest in their work, and although their methods may not always have met with approval from those in authority, they deserve every credit for their efforts to make the music an effective contribution to the service. There are still in existence old manuscript books, over a century old, which are models of neat and careful writing, and which bear testimony to the general desire to have tunes that should be acceptable to all who joined in sacred song.

Early Methodist Services.

In the *Arminian Magazine* for 1796 a writer, signing himself Disney Alexander (probably an assumed name) contributed a series of articles called ' Reasons for Methodism.' Describing the ' Mode of performing Divine Service among the Methodists,' he says : ' The service commences with singing, in which the greatest part of the congregation joins. The preacher next makes an extemporary prayer, and after a few more verses of an hymn have been sung, the sermon follows, which is likewise delivered extempore. The people now join in another hymn, and the whole is concluded with a prayer and blessing from the minister.' He adds, ' There are few devotional exercises which more powerfully raise the soul to God than the singing of psalms. When the language of an hymn is poetical, fluent and intelligible, when the sentiments expressed in it are truly pious and scriptural, the music solemn, and the people serious and earnest, I know of no employment better calculated to excite awful impressions of the Divinity, and to stir up our minds to a closer communion with God.' He concludes by saying that ' the hymns used in the Methodist chapels appear to me in a peculiar manner to have this effect.'

CHAPTER VI

THE USE OF STRINGED INSTRUMENTS

THE enthusiasm with which the singers rendered their anthems or ' set pieces,' as they were then called, did not meet with any enthusiastic reception from the Methodist preachers. They did not like them. Too much time, they said, was taken up by the music, and there was an undue proportion of it, notably at special services, when singers gathered from far and near to contribute to the harmony of the occasion.

At last official notice was taken of the matter, and at the Conference held at City Road Chapel in 1800 the subject of music was thus referred to :

Q. 15. Can anything be done to prevent what appears to us to be a great evil, namely, Bands of Music and Theatrical Singers being brought into our chapels, when charity sermons are to be preached?

A. Let none in our Connexion preach charity sermons where such persons and such music are introduced. And let the Stewards, Trustees and Leaders be informed that such a practice is offensive to the Conference, who believe it has been hurtful to the minds of many pious people.

Not only were the occupiers of the singers' pew in many chapels eager to extend their choral activities beyond the range of the ordinary hymn-tune, but the congregations appreciated the anthem, or ' set-piece,' as it was then called. Music of this kind was not lacking, for in addition to Handel's choruses and anthems by Kent, Mason, and others, contemporary composers were also writing music that met with great popularity. It is certain that these ' set-pieces ' and the singing of solos in chapels greatly vexed the older preachers, one of whom, some years later, thus expressed his feelings :

Some who have a taste for music, perhaps, and also a taste for worldly show, are willing to patronize the system of theatrical singing in places of worship; and thus it happens, that even in the present day, in many chapels, such exhibitions frequently occur. Very recently we heard of a young female singing solos in one of the chapels of a London circuit! (*Life of Adam Clarke.*)

It would appear that these Conference Resolutions did not have the desired effect, and special music continued to form a prominent item in many places. At the opening of Bridge Street Wesleyan Chapel, Bolton, by the Rev. Samuel Bradburn in 1803, the choir had arranged to sing as their anthem ' The horse and his rider hath He thrown into the sea.' This was duly performed with trumpets, horns, violins, hautboys, bassoons, bass viols and double bass, to the obvious delight of the performers, but the equally evident annoyance of the preacher. At length he could stand it no longer, and, turning to the eager musicians he exclaimed in a voice of amazing power : ' I say! put that horse in the stable; we've had enough of him for one day.' The astonished musicians promptly subsided, quite overawed for the time by the preacher's voice and manner.

The Bass Viol.

In 1805, at Sheffield, the Conference again dealt with the question of music. It is evident that some of the previous resolutions had not had the desired effect, and consequently the regulations became still more stringent.

Q. 20. Are there regulations necessary with regard to singing?

A. 1. Let no instruments of music be introduced into the singers' seats, except a bass viol, should the principal singer require it.

2. Let no books of hymns be henceforth used in our chapels, except the hymn-books printed for our Book-Room.

3. Let no *Pieces,* as they are called, in which *recitatives,* by single men, *solos,* by single women, *fuguing* (or different words sung by different voices at the same time) are introduced, be sung in our chapels.

4. Let the original, simple, grave and devotional style be carefully preserved, which, instead of drawing the attention to singing and the singers, is so admirably calculated to draw off the attention from both, and to raise the soul to God only.

5. Let no musical Festivals, or, as they are sometimes termed, *Selections of Sacred Music,* be either encouraged or permitted in any

THE USE OF STRINGED INSTRUMENTS

of our chapels: in which performances the genuine dignity of spiritual worship is grossly abused under the pretence of getting money for charitable purposes; which, we have sufficient proof, has been procured as amply where nothing of the kind has been introduced, but the charity recommended to the people in the name of God.

7. Let no Preacher, therefore, suffer his right to conduct every part of the worship of Almighty God to be infringed on, either by the singers or others.

From the above we gather that the only instrument allowed in Methodist chapels in addition to an organ was a bass viol, ' should the principal singer require it.' It is evident that the brethren who then assembled in Conference did not invite the assistance of a musician in framing their regulations, hence the distinction they drew between ' recitative ' and ' solo ' is scarcely in accordance with the generally accepted meanings of those terms. Equally mysterious is their idea of ' fuguing,' which they appear to have adopted without examination from John Wesley's ideas on the subject.

Objection to Fiddles.

It is not surprising to find that the licence given by Conference to the presence of a bass viol in the singing pew led to other instruments being gradually introduced. When Queen Street Chapel, Huddersfield, was first opened the singing was accompanied by a carefully selected band of stringed instruments. Some of the members of the congregation strongly objected to the violins, though they readily acquiesced in the use of the big fiddles, especially as they were permitted by Conference. They maintained that the squeak of the fiddle was entirely out of place in the sanctuary, being far too suggestive of the sounds that frequently proceeded from less hallowed places.

A discussion on the subject was subsequently started in the Quarterly Meeting, and supporters and opponents of the fiddle expressed their candid opinion of the instrument without any reserve. There was at that time a notable member of the congregation, Abraham Moss by name, known familiarly as ' owd

Abe Moss,' whose renown as a local preacher was great and far extended. The good man was appealed to for a decision on the subject. He replied, ' If t' fiddle is a sinner he's nobbut a little 'un. T' double bass is t' big sinner, an' if eyther on 'em is to be turned out o' choir it ought to be t' big sinner.'

This summing-up proved to be very satisfactory to all concerned. ' T' big sinner ' was there by authority, so he could not be banished, and thus it happened that the fiddle players were allowed to retain their places in the orchestra.

A historic 'cello or bass viol was the one that belonged to the old Mulberry St. Chapel in Sheffield. When that building was closed the instrument was handed over to the newly-erected Norfolk Street Chapel. The Rev. T. A. Seed, in his *History* of the building tells us that the old bow had done such good service that it had to be replaced by a new one at a cost of 8s. 2d.

CHAPTER VII

THE CHAPEL ORCHESTRA

THERE was also another instrument in active use, too insignificant, perhaps, to find a place in Conference Resolutions, but a very present help to the choirmaster, or chief singer. The pitch-pipe was much in evidence in those chapels and churches where no musical instrument was available. It was a small wooden pipe in which a movable stopper was inserted. The pipe was furnished with a mouthpiece, and by moving the stopper in or out any desired note could be obtained.

The pitch-pipe certainly had its uses. It enabled the leader to vary to a slight extent the key in which the tune was originally written, thereby avoiding the risk of carrying the singers beyond what they could comfortably compass. The setting of a tune without some such helpful guide not infrequently led to disaster, for the gift of correct pitch was possessed by few. It is on record how the Rev. Richard Watson was about to give out the first hymn at a week-evening service in a Lancashire village when he was asked to wait for a few moments as ' Betty, the tune-striker, had not yet arrived.'

On another occasion the Rev. J. H. Norton was conducting a similar service. The hymn before the service was of a somewhat unusual metre, and for a short time no one ventured to strike up. At last a woman bravely started a tune which nobody knew but herself. However, she was in no wise disconcerted, and carried the hymn to a more or less successful termination. By a peculiar coincidence the text of the minister's discourse was founded on the words ' She hath done what she could.'

A Village Precentor.

Some years ago the Rev. William Backhouse gave in a Christmas number of *The Methodist Recorder* the interesting portrait of an old-time village precentor:

STORIES OF METHODIST MUSIC

' There stood Peter Gorman, who, long before any musical instrument appeared, started the tunes. He was a prominent figure, an eccentric character, and an old local preacher. His small round head was nearly bald, except a solitary tuft on the top. He was an inveterate smoker, always using a long clay pipe, both indoors and out. He sought to compensate for his shortness of stature by standing on tiptoe. This was his attitude as he led the singing—his thumbs in his waistcoat arm-holes, standing on tip-toe, and beating time by dropping on his heels with a heavy thud, which formed an energetic accompaniment to the jerking tones of his sonorous voice. Often he proceeded without singing the words, but uttering meaningless sounds instead. Not seldom he commenced a wrong metre, or pitched the right tune too high, and after bravely struggling with it for a while, was compelled to abandon the attempt and begin again. But how the people did sing! There was something magnificent in the heartiness and vigour with which they sang such a hymn as

> How weak the thoughts, and vain
> Of self-deluding man;

to the old tune " Eccles." As they gave vent to their exultant feelings in the words

> Stands our city on a rock,
> On the Rock of heavenly love,

they almost seemed to shake the walls. And one can picture them, and see Peter Gorman leading them with his thumbs in the arm-holes of his vest, standing on tip-toe and ever thudding on the floor with his heels.'

The use of the pitch-pipe survived for many years, and there are some still living who have heard its note giving the signal. Some sixty years ago the singing at St. Sampson's Wesleyan Chapel, Guernsey, was led by an elderly gentleman with a stentorian voice. He had a curious black box containing eight pitch-pipes made of metal, and tuned from middle C to the octave above. After the hymn had been announced and the first two lines read (for hymns were at that time always given out two lines at a time) a shrill blast from one of the pipes would sound forth, giving the key-note of the tune, and the choir, taking it up, would promptly get the hymn under weigh.

The Bassoon.

It is only by diligent search through old circuit books that we can obtain definite information about the musical instruments in use in Methodist chapels a century ago. The task is not an easy one, for at the very commencement careful inquiry frequently elicits the fact that the old records have either been destroyed, or preserved in so negligent a way that they are torn and soiled to such an extent as to be almost indecipherable. Occasionally, however, one meets with a few interesting items, and these well deserve recording.

The Rev. Albert H. Walker, of Manchester, sends the following interesting note, which must find a place in this record :

' In making the gift of the old original Hadfield land and Wesleyan Chapel, near Glossop, in the year 1816, the donor, Mr. John Thornley, made this curious covenant with the trustees, viz. '' Provided also that the trustees for the time being shall not permit or suffer any musical instruments to be used in the said chapel except *One Bassoon* or *Bass-viol,* unless when a sermon or sermons is or are preached for the benefit of a Sunday School, or other charitable institution conducted by the members of the Methodist Society in or near Hadfield aforesaid, or for the purpose of making a public collection for the general support and carrying on of the work of God; and on these occasions such other instruments only shall be used as the superintendent preacher for the time being shall direct.'' '

The Serpent.

Another instrument that frequently figured in the orchestra or in the singing-pew was the serpent. This was a curious-looking instrument made of wood twisted into a curved shape and covered with thin leather. It was furnished with a mouth-piece, and arranged along the tube were keys for producing the different notes. It looked quite capable of giving forth full, deep sounds, but in reality the tone was somewhat subdued, entirely belieing both its name and its appearance. It is interesting to remember that this instrument has been used by all the great composers from Handel to Wagner. Handel originally scored for it in his Water Music, but afterwards erased the part, possibly because he could not find any one in England competent to play it. The great composer does not seem to have had a very favourable opinion of the instrument, and it is said that on one occasion he affirmed that it could not possibly have been the serpent that tempted Eve. Mendelssohn was more favourably disposed towards it. He employed it in his *Meerstille* overture, and also in the overture to *St. Paul*. When, however, the oratorio was to be given for the first time in London the town was ransacked for a competent performer, but none could be found, so the part was played on the instrument now known as the bombardon. In a letter from Paris written in 1832, Mendelssohn affirmed that the effect of the music at the church of St. Sulpice, accompanied by the serpent, was so fine as to be scarcely conceivable. Amongst other composers who have written for it are Beethoven, in his *March in D* for a military band; Rossini, in his overture to the *Siege of Corinth;* Auber, in *Masaniello,* and Wagner, who makes use of it in *Rienzi,* and (according to Prout) in *The Lovefeast of the Apostles.*

CHAPTER VIII

TROUBLE WITH THE SINGERS

REFERENCE has already been made to the occasional differences that unfortunately arose in some Methodist chapels over the music. The singers were not always ready or willing to recognize or acknowledge the authority of the pulpit. They could not bring themselves to forego their special music and their set pieces, and frequently the preacher found himself powerless to resist. But not always; sometimes he proved to be more than a match for them.

Samuel Bradburn had trouble with his singers when he was at Wakefield. The tunes they introduced into the service were such as he felt to be wholly unsuited to a place of worship, and the characters of some of the singers who assisted at the Sunday services were not such as would stand strict investigation. Finally he decided to adopt extreme measures. After entering the pulpit one evening he said to his congregation, ' You are, perhaps, surprised to see the singing-gallery empty. The fact is I have nailed up the door. I have borne with these fellows long enough, and am resolved to bear with them no longer. They shall either conduct the singing in a manner different from what they have done, or they shall not conduct it at all.'

The Singing Pew.

It is a fact well known to present-day choirmasters that when a singer has once established what he conceives to be his right place in the singing pew it is a serious thing to attempt to dislodge him. Still more serious is it when the whole choir find themselves dispossessed of their tenement. A choir had been formed at the Plymouth Dock Chapel, and the members thereof had set their hearts on occupying a particular pew, which they proposed to use as the singing-seat. Unfortunately it had been previously engaged by a private individual, and the trustees declined to evict him, suggesting that the singers ought to be satisfied with the seat allotted to them, which happened to be the best in the building. However, they refused to be satisfied, and took a curious way of showing their displeasure. The preacher for the day was the celebrated Adam Clarke, and when he had given out his first hymn he waited for the singers to begin; but as no sound arose from that quarter, he assumed that they had not heard the number of the hymn, so he gave it out again. Still they kept silence, and the good Doctor was obliged to raise the tune himself. The same process was gone through with the other hymns, the choir maintaining a stony silence throughout the service. It was just the same in the evening, but before the next Sunday the trustees engaged a precentor to pitch the tunes, and the choir found their occupation gone.

Conference Regulates the Singing.

In many cases, however, the will of the singers prevailed, and the preacher found himself powerless to resist. He certainly had the power and the right to appeal to Conference, and there at any rate he met with moral support, and possibly a certain amount of practical sympathy, which once again found expression in the following terms at the Manchester Conference of 1815, and which I give in full in order to make the story complete.

Q. 15. What directions are necessary with respect to our congregational singing?

A. 1. Let no singing be allowed in any of our chapels after the public service has been regularly closed by the officiating Preacher; as we think that singing, at such times, tends to extinguish the spirit of devotion, and to destroy those serious impressions which may have been made on the congregations by the previous ministry of God's word.

2. Let our rules respecting singing, and especially those which restrict the use of instrumental music in our public worship, as published in our Minutes for the year 1805, be uniformly enforced.

3. Let the excellent paper, inserted by Mr. Wesley in the *Arminian Magazine* for 1781, and entitled 'Thoughts on the Power of Music,' be immediately reprinted in the Magazine, and also published in a separate form, that copies may be sent to every Circuit. And let the Preachers promote, as much as possible, the restoration (in our public singing) of the style of music which that paper recommends, and which is exemplified in many of our best and oldest tunes.

4. Let our Preachers take care to examine the hymns which are to be sung in our chapels, when charity-sermons are to be preached, or on other particular occasions; and let them reject all those which are not decidedly unobjectionable in point of sentiment and of poetry. And we earnestly recommend that our own authorized hymns be generally preferred for all such purposes.

Wesley's article on music was duly reprinted in the *Methodist Magazine* for November 1815.

The Hymn-Book question was again raised in 1816 at London, in these terms :

The Conference recommend to our congregations, on the Lord's-day forenoon, the use of the Psalms and Hymns, first collected by Mr. Wesley, enlarged by Dr. Coke, and now used in some of our chapels in London.

The hymn-book here referred to was first published in 1784, with the title, ' A Collection of Psalms and Hymns for the Lord's Day.' After Wesley's death it was enlarged by Dr. Coke, and came to be used in the chapels where the Liturgy was read at the morning service, hence it was known as the ' Morning Hymn-Book.' Originally it contained one hundred and eighteen psalms and hymns, but various additions and alterations were made in successive editions. It passed out of use soon after 1830.

The Chained Harmonium.

But these occasional, yet none the less deplorable scenes of strife were not always caused by the singers who, as a rule, rendered invaluable service as leaders of church praise. Now and then a prominent member of the congregation would, perhaps unwittingly, cause strife by adopting autocratic methods. A story illustrating this concerns certain doings many years ago at a small village chapel in Hertfordshire. It has for its theme the coming and going of a harmonium.

One of the villagers, a somewhat overbearing and consequently unpopular member of the Methodist Society, was very anxious to introduce a harmonium into the chapel. His neighbours rather suspected that there was some private interest, possibly financial, behind his newly-acquired musical enthusiasm. However, they yielded to his persuasions, and agreed that the instrument might be introduced on trial.

It was soon found that the change was unacceptable, and the good man was requested to remove it. This he absolutely refused to do, saying that by admitting it on chapel premises the trustees had become purchasers, and were responsible for payment. The trustees retorted by saying that if he did not remove it within a certain time, the offending instrument would be removed off the premises. When the congregation assembled on the following Sunday, they found the instrument fastened to the choir seats by a chain!

A day or two afterwards two or three members quietly went to the chapel, filed through the chain, and conveyed the instrument to the enemy's house. Finding it shut up, they deposited their burden on the doorstep, where the unhappy victim found it when he returned home. Highly indignant, he promptly sought the aid of the law, but lost his case on a technical point.

CHAPTER IX

CONFERENCE REGULATIONS ABOUT MUSIC

ALTHOUGH Wesley, as we have already seen, appears to have raised no formidable objection to the introduction of an organ into his preaching-houses, it is very certain that the great majority of his brethren did not agree with this. At the same time there is no doubt that the Conference was thoroughly in earnest in its endeavour to secure what they considered to be the most effective form of worship-music, and we find that the subject is again dealt with at some length three years later at Bristol (1808).

Q. 18. What directions are necessary respecting public worship?

A. 2. We desire that all our Preachers will strongly urge on their congregations the propriety and importance of standing while they sing the praises of God.

3. The Conference judge it expedient to refuse after this present year their sanction or consent to the erection of any organs in our chapels.

4. Where organs have been already introduced, the Conference require that they shall be so used as not to overpower or supersede, but only to assist our congregational singing; and that they shall be considered as under the control of the Superintendent or of the officiating Preacher for the time being, whose right and duty it is to conduct every part of the public worship of God. Let no voluntaries be played during the time of divine service; and let all the rules respecting singing and instrumental music which were made at the Sheffield Conference in 1805 and published in the Minutes of that year, be uniformly enforced.

The First Organs in Liverpool.

The strong feeling exhibited by Conference against the erection of organs did not meet with the approval of certain musical enthusiasts, and a small instrument was surreptitiously introduced into the new chapel in Pitt Street, Liverpool. However, ' a fermentation took place,' as Joseph Everett says in his *Diary*, and it was promptly taken to pieces and removed.

STORIES OF METHODIST MUSIC

When Brunswick Chapel, Liverpool, was built in 1811 there was a strong desire expressed for an organ, and accordingly the officials and their friends petitioned the Conference of that year to grant permission for its erection. This was a poser. Although the Conference were not prepared to go back on their ruling, they were equally unwilling to disoblige their Liverpool friends. The question was solemnly debated for half a day, and when at last the voting was taken it was found that the organ-lovers had a majority of seventy-four in their favour, certainly a notable victory. Here is the letter conveying the consent of Conference :

SHEFFIELD,

August 3, 1811.

VERY DEAR BRETHREN,—We are desired by the Conference to send you the most speedy information in respect to the erection of an organ in your new chapel. The Conference have very fully and calmly debated on the subject ; the report of their committee on your business was very fully considered ; four hours were employed on this important business ; when the whole debate was closed the judgement of the Conference was taken by ballot. The report of the committee included the following resolutions, viz. that considering the local circumstances of Brunswick Chapel, Liverpool, our rule concerning organs shall be so far suspended that Brunswick Chapel shall be considered as an exempt case, and that the Conference will not oppose the erection of an organ there under the following restrictions, viz. that the organ be constructed on the simplest plan and with such stops as will be useful to assist in congregational singing, that there be no voluntaries, that the organist shall be a Methodist, that he shall exercise his office under the directions of the officiating preacher, that he shall be movable at the direction of the superintendent, and that neither his salary nor any contingent expenses which may result from the use of the organ shall be paid out of the funds of the society. When the votes were counted, the decision was : for the introduction of the organ in the new chapel at Liverpool, with the above instruction, 163, against it 89. We are authorized to inform you that the Conference felt exquisitely for the preservation of the general rule concerning organs, but the candid consent of the trustees in respect of the above restriction has prevailed on the Conference to grant their request.

C. ATMORE, *President.*

T. COKE, *Secretary.*

Thus it will be seen that there were to be no voluntaries, and the instrument was only to have such stops as were necessary for accompanying the hymns.

The fact that an organ had been allowed in a Liverpool chapel seems to have been kept very quiet, for it was more than once stated in pamphlets issued during the Leeds organ controversy that no organ had been erected in a Methodist chapel during the first twenty years of the nineteenth century.

Nine years later the Conference met at Liverpool, when many of those who attended would have the opportunity of hearing the organ in Brunswick Chapel in that town for the first time. It was probably silent during the meetings that were held, for the organ has never been used during the ordinary sittings of Conference. This rule holds good to this day, the tunes being ' pitched ' by the Precentor, who as such has an official position in that august assembly.

Conference Discussion about Organs.

At this Liverpool Conference we find the organ question once more under discussion, and new regulations for their introduction are given in answer to the query, ' What is the decision of the Conference on the erection of organs in our chapels? '

We think that in some of the larger chapels, where some instrumental music may be deemed expedient in order to guide the congregational singing, organs may be allowed, by special consent of the Conference, but every application for such consent shall be made first at the District Meeting; and, if it obtain their sanction, shall be then referred to a Committee at the Conference, who shall report their opinion as to the propriety of acceding to the request, and also as to the restrictions with which the permission to erect an organ ought, in that particular case, to be accompanied.

This resolution is of considerable importance, as it laid down a definite line of action for those who desired to have an organ to act upon. Apparently those who framed the resolution did not realize at the time how indefinite it was, or they would certainly have been a little more careful in their phraseology. But there was trouble ahead, and a few years later a crisis was reached, when an organ was about to be introduced in the Brunswick Chapel at Leeds.

Edward Booth.

A famous organist of this period was Edward Booth, one of the many notable church musicians that the north of England has produced. Born in 1798, he became a pupil of Hummel, a distinguished German musician, who paid several visits to this country. From his master Booth inherited a love of the music of the great composers, which he maintained throughout his long career. He was a man of quiet and retiring disposition, and produced but little in the way of original composition. His most notable work was the *Wesleyan Psalmody*, a large oblong collection of tunes which he published in 1843. A special feature was the thematic index, which gave the first line of each tune in the book. It was one of the most notable tune-books published in the last century, and it is somewhat remarkable that no small cheap edition was ever issued for choir use. In or about 1873, he issued a small number of tunes as a supplement to the larger work. He originally compiled it for use at Brunswick Chapel, Leeds, where he presided at the organ for upwards of forty years. The story of this famous instrument will now be related.

CHAPTER X

THE LEEDS ORGAN CASE

The Brunswick Organ.

A CENTURY ago Methodism in Leeds was divided into the West and the East circuits, the principal place of worship in the latter being Brunswick Chapel, which was opened in 1825. At that time it was the largest in the Connexion, and the Leeds Methodists were very proud of it, or at any rate, those of the East circuit were.

But there were some who were not altogether satisfied. A fear was expressed that a more elaborate service might be introduced, and it has been stated that some subscribers to the building made it a condition of their contributions that no organ should be introduced. The chapel was well attended, the congregations increased, and everything promised well. Then some of the trustees took counsel amongst themselves, and came to the conclusion that if an organ were introduced it would greatly assist the congregation in their singing. The idea was well received by many of the congregation, and the trustees, thus encouraged, discussed the question at a properly summoned Trustees' Meeting, when it was decided, by a small majority, that an organ should be erected. Those who had the scheme in hand were much encouraged by the receipt of a petition from nine-tenths of the pew-holders, requesting that the organ should be erected. Steps were at once taken to carry out the work, and the building of the instrument was entrusted to Joseph Booth, of Wakefield.

Trouble Begins.

Signs of dissent soon began to arise, and it is a curious fact that the first suggestions of disapproval came from members, chiefly local preachers, who belonged to the neighbouring West circuit, and who really had no right or claim to any voice in the matter. The Leaders' Meetings in both circuits disapproved of an organ, and took great pains to say so. Why the West circuit folk, who worshipped at the Old Chapel (formerly known as the Boggart) should have interfered with their neighbours one is at a loss to know. Besides, they had several instruments, forming a band, at the Old Chapel, and why should they grudge Brunswick the possession of a single instrument?

But arguments like these were of no avail. The opposition to the Brunswick organ increased daily, and its opponents demanded that the decision of Conference as to the erection of organs in Methodist chapels should be strictly adhered to.

We have already seen in a previous chapter that in 1820 the Conference decided that ' organs may be allowed, by special consent of Conference, but every application for such consent shall be first made at the District Meeting, and if it obtain their sanction shall then be referred to a Committee at the Conference, who shall report their opinion as to the propriety of acceding to the request.'

The District Meeting's Refusal.

In February 1827 the trustees began to invite subscriptions for the organ; also, to strengthen their case, they made application to the District Meeting to sanction the organ, and encountered an adverse vote. They at once intimated their intention to appeal to a higher court, namely, to Conference, and received permission to do so. This greatly aroused the wrath of their opponents, who considered that the veto of the District Meeting was final. The law is certainly somewhat ambiguous, as laws frequently are, but the opposing party protested against any appeal being made, and called a public meeting to air their views. Herein lay their undoing. For thirty years previously Conference had forbidden any member of the Connexion to call any such meeting.

Conference Consents.

The trustees carried their case to Conference, and it was duly considered by a Committee, who reported in favour of the scheme, and so the trustees finally obtained official sanction for the erection of their organ. But this by no means ended the dispute.

THE LEEDS ORGAN CASE

Numerous pamphlets were issued, setting forth the various aspects of the case, and a perusal of some of these gives a strange insight into the wondrous storm that arose round this organ. As the dispute waxed fiercer and fiercer other issues were raised, and in the end the original cause of the disturbance was well-nigh forgotten.

Opening of the Organ.

Meanwhile the organ was being built by Booth, and it was dispatched from his works at Wakefield in August 1828. There had been so much talk about the instrument that, as the time drew near for the opening, public curiosity was greatly aroused, and people were asking who was going to open it. Their question was answered by a paragraph in the *Leeds Mercury,* September 6, 1828, to this effect :

ORGANS AND ORGANISTS. The organ at Brunswick Chapel in this town, which has already made so much noise in the world, is announced to be opened on Friday next by Charles Wesley, the celebrated performer, and the services of the day promise to be of a very interesting and attractive kind.

It is true that Charles Wesley, eldest surviving son of the hymn-writer, was first approached, but he was of a rather indolent disposition. He did not approve of long coach journeys, nor did he like being away from home. Also he had just lost his beloved sister, who had been his constant companion for many years. So he got his brother Samuel to take his place, and there was much uncertainty in Leeds as to who was really coming, for all the information the *Leeds Intelligencer* (September 11, 1828) could give to its readers was that ' A Mr. Wesley is on his way to Leeds. He slept at Nottingham last night, and will be here to-day.'

In the same paper is a description of the new instrument, from which we learn that it occupied nearly the whole of the space from the front of the singing gallery to the wall in the rear. The case was of mahogany, with a gorgeous display of gilt pipes at the front and on the two sides, whilst four carved ornaments surmounted the whole. The instrument originally had thirty

4

stops, but there is no record in existence of the names, except that one was ' a double open diapason, such as is not to be found on any other organ in this part of the country, the effect of which is said to be truly sublime.'

An elaborate invitation card was issued, which informed its recipients that there would be three services on the day of opening, the preachers being Robert Newton, W. M. Bunting, and Theophilus Lessey. There was a considerable amount of money still to be raised, and the trustees put the matter very neatly on the invitation card thus: ' For the better accommodation of the congregation, and those friends who may attend on this occasion, the trustees have thought it desirable that silver shall be taken at the entrance to the gallery, and the pews, and in the body of the chapel.' Arrangements were made for the poor, who were provided with free seats.

Samuel Wesley gave short organ recitals before the morning and evening services, and the choir showed their skill in the singing of selected choruses. There appears to be no record in existence of what the music given on this famous occasion consisted. The services were well attended, and the collections on the day of opening and following Sunday amounted to £260, which was certainly remarkable, when we remember the difficulties that attended the scheme. The cost of the instrument was eight hundred guineas.

CHAPTER XI

MORE ABOUT HYMN-BOOKS

Faithful Choristers.

THERE is no indication that the trouble caused by the introduction of the organ at Brunswick Chapel, Leeds, spread to any other part of the Connexion. One of the London circuits manifested a slight interest, but that was all. There is plenty of evidence to show that during the second and third decades of last century and even later, Methodist choirs were taking their work very seriously, and in most places their services were greatly appreciated. For instance, at the opening of Fletcher Street Chapel, Bolton, the trustees, instead of providing a dinner for the singers, made them a grant of £7, and then, fearing that such an amount might not go far enough, or, as the resolution said, ' might not be sufficient to accommodate them with eating, &c.' the kind-hearted trustees added another sovereign, and also granted the full use ' of the old chapel vestry and plates and other utensils.'

The feast was duly held, and the bill for the same (apparently not audited) shows that the musicians kept well within their limits, in spite of the disappointment over 'the beer that was bad.'

	£	s.	d.
Beer	1	3	11
Mutton, 20 lbs. at 8d.	0	13	4
Beef, 59¼ lbs. at 7d.	1	14	6
Bread, 61 lbs. at 2d.	0	10	2
Cheese, 8½ lbs. at 8d.	0	5	8
Potatoes	0	3	0½
Carriage on the Potatoes	0	0	3
Water	0	0	6
Tea	0	2	7
Sugar	0	5	8½
Pepper	0	0	2

Salt	...	...	...	...	...	...	...	...	0	1	2
Mustard	...	...	...	...	...	...	...	...	0	0	5
Vinegar	...	...	...	...	...	...	...	...	0	0	8
Butter	...	...	...	...	...	...	...	...	0	5	6½
Six Quarts of Milk at 3d.		...	...	...	...	...			0	1	6

			5	9 1½
Balance	...	...	...	...	2 10 10½

	£8	0 0
Balance from the other side	...	2 10 10½
Cash returned on account of loss on beer that was bad ...	...	0 7 10½
	£2	3 0

The New Hymn-Book of 1831.

The collection of hymns bequeathed by John Wesley was in general use in Methodist chapels for forty years after his death. Slight alterations were occasionally made, and irresponsible publishers tried hard to pass off 'pirate' editions on unsuspecting purchasers, but all to no purpose. It was not until 1830 that the necessity of issuing a new and duly authorized hymn-book had become urgent, owing to the fact that the copyright of the 1780 hymn-book had terminated. The manuscripts of Charles Wesley's hymns had been in the possession of the family since his death, and in 1830 several of them passed by purchase into the possession of the Wesleyan Conference. Thus the copyright was secured in a 'Supplement' to the original hymn-book, which was bound up with the 1780 book, and this new collection became the authorized hymn-book for 'the use of the people called Methodists.' The task of preparing this Supplement was entrusted to J. Bunting, R. Watson and T. Jackson. These three divines were not agreed as to the merits of many of Watts' hymns. Jackson considered them ' often careless, feeble, and unevangelical,' but his associates thought otherwise, and so Watts' productions found many a resting-place in the new book, where Jackson would have preferred to install Charles Wesley.

This book was published early in 1831, and at the Liverpool Conference of 1832, the following suggestion was made:

MORE ABOUT HYMN-BOOKS

As it appears that in a few of the Circuits the Supplement to our Hymn-Book has not yet been introduced, it is the judgement of the Conference that its adoption in our public worship ought to be universal, as greatly tending to the spiritual edification of our people: it is therefore directed that the Supplement be used with the large Hymn-Book in all our chapels.

A Revised ‘ Sacred Harmony.’

The introduction of this new hymn-book brought in its train a very larger number of tune-books of all kinds and shapes. Many of them were the productions of local musicians, most of whom usually acted as leaders of the singing in their respective places of worship. But in some quarters the demand had already been anticipated. In 1822 a new edition of *Sacred Harmony* was issued from the Conference office under the editorship of Charles Wesley, eldest surviving son of the poet. The form of the book —a small oblong volume—was quite different from the earlier editions, and contained a Preface in which the editor expressed his admiration for the old psalm-tunes, and denounced in strong terms contemporary collections of tunes which ‘ deluged the Connexion with base, dissonant, unscientific, and tasteless compositions,’ and he went on to blame the ministers themselves for allowing such things to be. But in spite of his protest new tune-books continued to be issued, and it is to this period that we trace such tunes as ‘ Sagiora ’ and compositions by W. Matthews, T. Jarman, J. Newton, John Fawcett, and others.

The Centenary of Methodism.

There are two collections of tunes belonging to this era which deserve special mention. In 1839 the centenary of the commencement of Methodism was celebrated, and in connexion with that event a *Centenary Tune-Book* was published, which has a curious history. The preface is dated from Liverpool (December 1839). It is unsigned, and no hint is given as to who was responsible for the collection. There is every reason to believe that the compiler designed his collection primarily for use at Brunswick Chapel, Liverpool. He certainly produced a very attractive volume, but it seems to have had a very limited sale, and copies are now very scarce. It would appear that the compiler unwittingly infringed some copyrights, and thought it better to avoid the consequences by withdrawing the book from publication. More than fifty years after the same title was used for a collection of ' Old Methodist Tunes.'

The ' Companion.'

The other collection dating from the same period had a much longer career, and was to some extent a semi-official publication. It was called *The Companion to the Wesleyan Hymn-Book,* and bore the imprint of the Wesleyan Conference office. Issued about 1841, it had a long spell of popularity, which it certainly well deserved. No editor's name appears, but it is stated in the preface that ' the work originated in a private manuscript collection of tunes prepared for the use of a small country congregation.' A special feature is a detailed account of the various metres dealt with, which certainly provided interesting and instructive reading for the intelligent singer. The collection was frequently bound up with the hymn-book, and in this form it was issued as late as 1873. It would appear that Methodist congregations had their first insight into the mysteries of chanting through using the *Companion*. At the end of the book some excellent instructions are given for performing this pleasing, though somewhat difficult act of worship.

CHAPTER XII

RECENT DEVELOPMENTS

The Law About Organs.

AFTER the close of the Leeds organ affair Conference held its peace as regards musical matters till sixteen years had elapsed. The subject was once more discussed at Birmingham in 1844, when new rules were enacted to provide for the erection of organs in Methodist chapels. These rules were confirmed at Bristol two years later, and after that the conditions were crystallized in the following resolution adopted at Leeds in 1866:

> Every application for permission to introduce an Organ into a Chapel shall be made, on the Schedule provided for the purpose, to the District Committee, or District Chapel Sub-Committee; and, if it obtain their approval, shall then be submitted to the Chapel Committee. The entire cost of an Organ shall be defrayed at or before the opening.

No further additions have been made to these regulations since 1866, and the conditions they contain have still to be observed when it is proposed to erect an organ in a Methodist place of worship.

Giving out the Hymn.

For many years much diversity of opinion existed as to the best way of announcing and singing the hymn. Conference took the matter up in 1844, and decided the matter thus:

> MODE OF GIVING OUT HYMNS. Complaints having been made that, in some of our chapels, the novel practice has been introduced of reading and singing a whole verse of a hymn at once, instead of our usual and regular plan of giving out successive portions of verses, the Conference hereby records its serious disapproval of this innovation, as being inconvenient and injurious, especially to the poorer classes of our fellow-worshippers, and not generally conducive to edification.

The system of giving out two lines at a time met with John

Wesley's approval, and the custom prevailed well into the nineteenth century. The singers did not like it, though it is evident that the ministers did. But the giving-out of a whole verse still prevailed in some places especially where there were no instruments to help the voices to sustain the pitch. At the London Conference of 1860 another attempt was made to keep up the custom of giving out the hymn two lines at a time, and the following appears amongst the Miscellaneous Resolutions :

LINING OF HYMNS. Resolved, that the Conference hears with regret of increasingly numerous cases of departure from our long-established custom of giving out the verse in successive portions; not only because that practice appears to be more conducive than any other to the ends of devotion, especially on the part of the poor, but also because any interference with our ordinary modes of worship is on many accounts undesirable. And, while unwilling to urge the discontinuance of the latter practice where it has long existed, the Conference instructs the Ministers of the Body to discourage, by all prudent means, its introduction in other places.

But this pious resolution availed little. The ' verse ' system continued to flourish, and gradually gave way to the present custom of giving out the first verse only, which may be said to date from about 1890. It is now well-nigh universal.

The modern history of Methodist music dates from 1876, when a new hymn- and tune-book was prepared by order of the Conference. It proved a great success, and its use resulted in a wonderful and much needed improvement in congregational singing. The committee responsible for its production encountered many obstacles. Two of the music editors, H. J. Gauntlett and George Cooper, died whilst the work was in progress, but the task of finishing was successfully carried out by E. J. Hopkins.

At the close of last century the question of a new hymn-book was being freely discussed, and in 1900 the Conference took the matter up, and appointed a Committee ' to make a selection of hymns for publication as a new Connexional Hymn-Book.' When their task was completed, another committee prepared the music edition under the guidance of Sir Frederick Bridge, as editor and adviser. The result of the united labours of these two committees was made public in 1904, when the *Methodist Hymn-Book* first came into use at the Sheffield Conference. The labours of Rev. Nehemiah Curnock as Secretary of the two committees well deserves to be put on permanent record here.

Sunday School Music.

Only once, apparently, did Conference attempt to regulate the music worship of the Sunday Schools. In 1844 directions were given ' that the Wesleyan Hymn-book shall be used in all schools now or hereafter to be connected with Wesleyan Methodism.' The framer of this resolution was not very exact in his description, for there never has been a collection of hymns bearing the above title. The name of the book in use from 1831 to 1876 was ' Wesley's Hymns,' but it is safe to assume that this was the collection referred to. Legislation for posterity is not an easy matter, and our spiritual advisers little thought that in years to come Methodist Sunday Schools would have a special hymn-book of their own.

In 1806 the Rev. Joseph Benson published *Hymns for Children and Young Persons,* and eight years later he published a revised edition called *Hymns for Children.* These were the first attempts to provide the children of Methodist families with a suitable collection of hymns, but there is no indication that either of them was designed for use in Sunday Schools. Two collections were published under the direction of the London Book Committee, the first in 1835, and the second in 1857, the latter being edited by Dr. W. H. Rule. A year later a tune-book was published as a companion to Dr. Rule's book. Many of us still remember the little oblong *Wesleyan Sunday School Hymn-Book,* with its blue cloth covers. Amongst the tunes it contained are ' Hark, the herald angels sing ' (Mendelssohn) which is probably its earliest appearance as a hymn-tune. In 1871 appeared the *Methodist Scholar's Tune-Book,* which provided Sunday Schools wth a more suitable choice of tunes. But the hymn-book connected with it did not please everybody, and in 1879 it was supplanted by *The Methodist Sunday School Hymn-*

Book, which was an excellent compilation, both as regards words and music. So good, indeed, was it, that it held the field for upwards of thirty years, when changed conditions brought about a demand for a new collection. This was issued in 1911 under the title of *The Methodist School Hymnal,* which has proved to be one of the best books of the kind ever issued.

The Conference Musical Festivals.

In recent years our governing body has again recognized the importance of music as an essential adjunct to church worship. In 1911 a notable addition was made to the series of public meetings held in connexion with the Conference by the institution of what has come to be known as the ' Conference Musical Festival.' It is ' the official recognition by the Wesleyan Methodist Conference of the value of music in church worship.'

These Festivals have been held each year since their institution (except in 1916 and 1917), and have gone on increasing in influence and indeed in popularity. The interest they have aroused has been widespread, so much so, in fact, that the number has been increased in recent years, two or three Festivals being held in various districts, whilst in 1927 no less than five were held in the West Riding of Yorkshire during the sessions of the Conference. Encouragement has also been given by the Methodist Church in another direction. In 1910 a new magazine was announced by the Methodist Publishing House under the name of *The Choir.* This successful and very helpful monthly periodical is devoted chiefly to the advancement of church music in its various forms, while many of its articles deal also with historical and educational matters.

In various other ways the interests of church music are being sustained and advanced by skilful organists and experienced choirmasters. The one thing needful at the present day is to insure that the music portion of our church worship shall be mainly directed to the advancement of congregational singing, thus sustaining the reputation which has marked the services in years gone by, and still makes them ' seasons of grace and sweet delight.'